Jesus Christ Return
Foreseen Peace

Michael P. Wright

Copyright © 2024 by Michael P. Wright
All rights reserved. No part of this book may be reproduced in any manner whatsoever without written permission except in the case of brief quotations embodied in critical articles and reviews.
First Printing, 2024

Jesus Christ Return

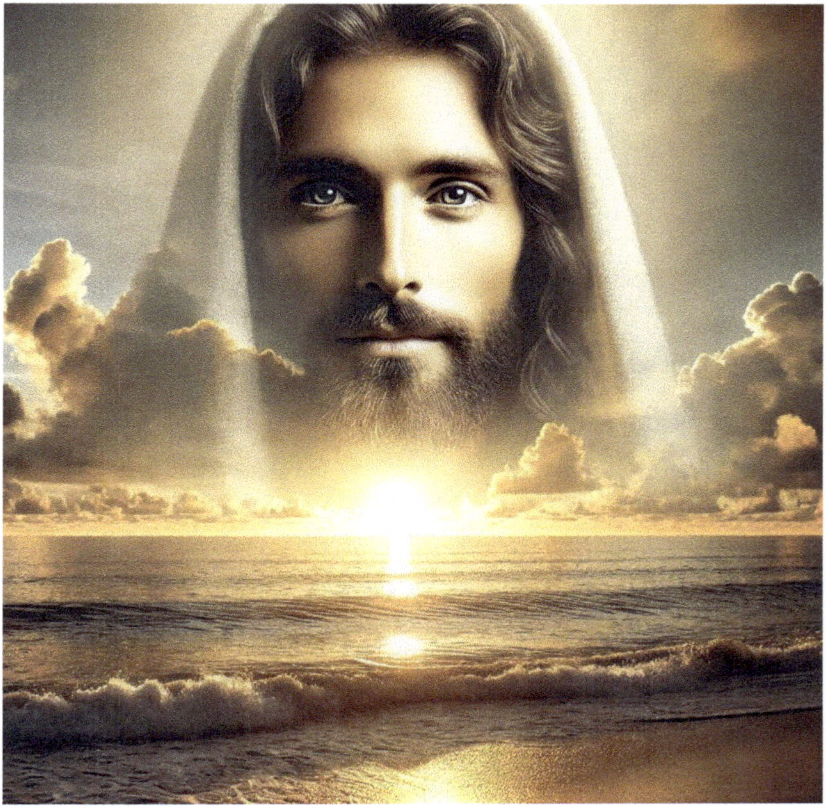

Contents

Photo Insert   v

Photo Insert   1

Text Insert   2

1 Chapter 1 – Present Day   3

2 Chapter 2 – World Chaos   5

3 Chapter 3 – Signs of the Times   7

4 Chapter 4 – Revelation   9

5 Chapter 5 – Where is Our Hope?   11

6 Chapter 6 – Future Changes in the World   13

7 Chapter 7 – Great Reset   15

8 Chapter 8 – Acceptance of Jesus Christ   17

9 Chapter 9 – Resistance of Jesus Christ   19

10 Chapter 10 - Pathway to Peace   21

11 Chapter 11 – Prince of Peace   23

12 Chapter 12 – Good Verse Evil   25

13 Chapter 13 – Jesus has Overcome the World   27

14	Chapter 14 – God's Law	29
15	Chapter 15 – Jesus the Redeemer	31
16	Chapter 16 – Light of the World	33
17	Chapter 17 – Unseen Eternity	35
18	Chapter 18 – Anti-Christ Rises	37
19	Chapter 19 – False Prophets	39
20	Chapter 20 – Mark of the Beast	41
21	Chapter 21 – Hidden Battle	43
22	Chapter 22 – End of the Age	45
23	Chapter 23 – Nation Against Nation	47
24	Chapter 24 – Shofar from Heaven	49
25	Chapter 25 – Breaking of the Seven Seals	51
26	Chapter 26 – Rapture	53
27	Chapter 27 – Tribulation	55
28	Chapter 28 – Holy One Verse Satan	57
29	Chapter 29 – Fall of the Beast	59
30	Chapter 30 – New Jerusalem	61
31	Chapter 31 – Author Living Testimony	65

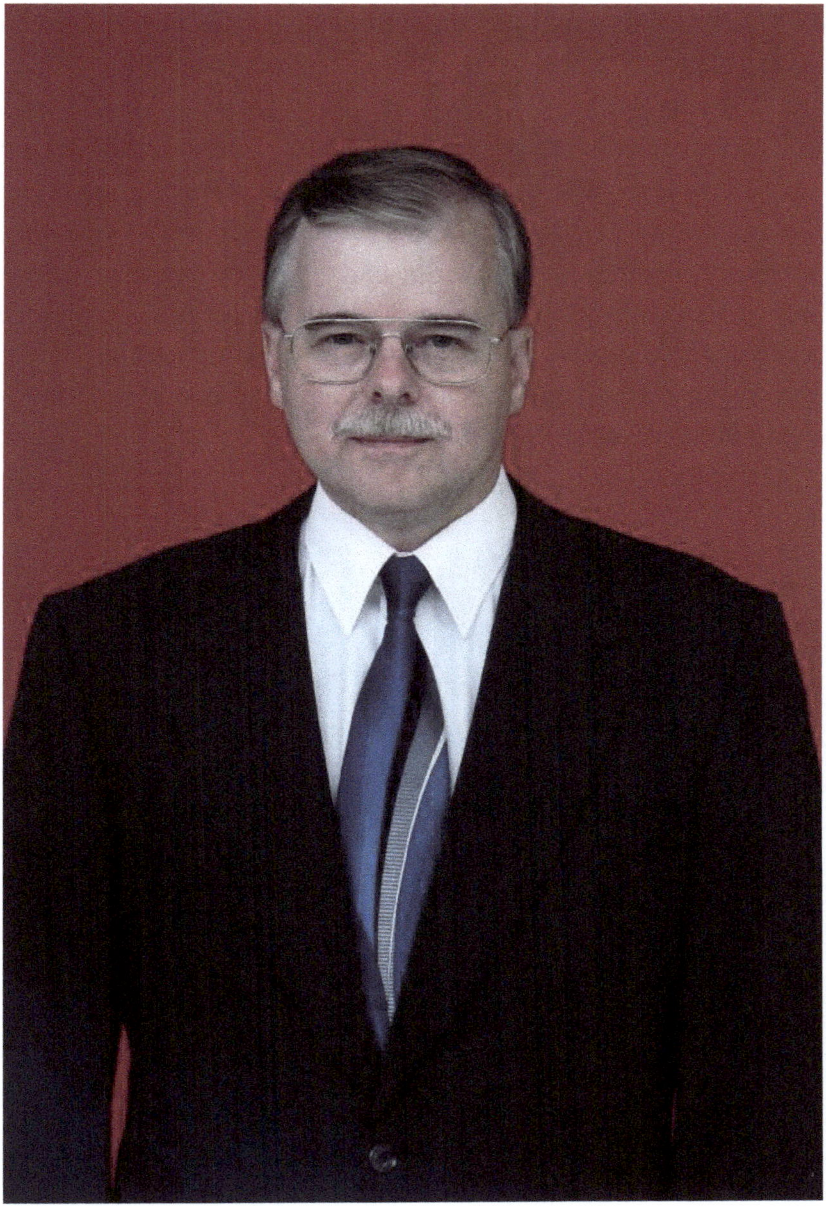

"For as lightning that comes from the east is visible even in the west, so will be the coming of the Son of Man."

Matthew 24:27

"And there will be signs in sun and moon and stars, and on the earth distress of nations in perplexity because of the roaring of the sea and the waves, people fainting with fear and with foreboding of what is coming on the world. For the powers of the heavens will be shaken. And then they will see the Son of Man coming in a cloud with power and great glory. Now when these things begin to take place, straighten up and raise your heads, because your redemption is drawing near."

Luke 21:25-28

A Book Inspired By God

Books – Launching Dates
September 2016 – The Next Great Crusade of Our Time
February 2017 – World Crusade Human Destiny
January 2018 – Middle East on Fire in the 21st Century
February 2019 – World Crusade in the 21st Century
November 2019 – Tenth Crusade of the World
November 2020 – God's Earth
December 2023 – God Overseer of Nature Climate Calamity
November 2024 – Jesus Christ Return Foreseen Peace

Chapter 1 – Present Day

With the global population at 8.1 billion people, researchers estimate 109 billion people have lived and died over the time of 192,000 years. For many thousands of years, there were fewer people on Earth that would live in a mid-sized city today. This dramatic increase in the world's human population is relatively new. It is these 109 billion people we have to thank for the civilization that we live in. The languages that we speak, the food we cook, the music we enjoy, the tools we use and what we know we learned from them.

It is hard to predict which path humanity will go down in the future, and how that will affect future population growth. It was only in 2007 that the majority of humans began to live in cities and in 2018 that the majority gained access to the internet. We will never meet the 109 billion humans who laid the foundation for our modern societies, we have never been more connected as a species.

Humanities future is at stake. Which deeply influential technology can we invest our current time in that will give humanity the tools to survive? How much time does humanity have left? The most vital societal challenge is to extend the longevity of humanity. Long term outcomes for humanity are connected to present day actions and global priorities. Science is what led our society to the present day.

Chapter 2 – World Chaos

Our world is in chaos. The increase in problems that our world is facing despite all the advances in science and medicine is overwhelming. The impact of human activity on the Earth system could result in unpredictable chaos from which there is no return. In a world where natural resources such as food, fuel and water are less accessible for millions, the potential for violent social unrest is ever present.

The world is in chaos because man has moved away from nature and has believed that they are the owners of this world. Man takes and continues to take from Mother Nature. Why are policymakers, scholars, and the general public so surprised when the world turns out to be unpredictable? World politics is at the edge of chaos. The more extreme end, Earth runs into havoc. This means that the planet's system evolves into chaotic behavior.

Humanity is on the edge of chaos. We have pushed our species and many others to the brink of extinction by misguided actions informed by a limited point of view. The internet is chaos and it is a reflection of humanity. The internet has become the woof of our global society. Social media is the technology that enables humans for good or bad unlike ever before. Where have we lost it that we should always fight? What has happened to our humanity?

Chapter 3 – Signs of the Times

In the very nature of things, the signs of the times will not cease until the Lord comes. The signs of the times in our day are events that were prophesied to take place in the latter days before the Second Coming of Christ. Through the prophets the Lord has revealed many signs that pertain to the dispensation to help latter-day Israel prepare for His Second Coming and the great events that will precede it. Those that involve chaos and distress of humanity will happen.

"But when you hear of wars and rumors of wars, do not be troubled; for such things must happen, but the end is not yet. For nation will rise against nation, and kingdom against kingdom. And there will be earthquakes in various places, and there will be famines and troubles. These are the beginnings of sorrows." These signs serve to remind the believer that history serves God's redemptive purposes in Christ; that the end of history is drawing near. (Matthew 24:6-8)

On the time-line of history, the signs of the times are understood often to be a cluster of events that will take place in a short period of time. The Bible is clear about the signs pointing to the last days, also known as the end times or the end of the age. World conditions as well as Bible chronology indicate that the days began in 1914, the year World War 1 began. In 1914 God's Kingdom began ruling in heaven and one of its first actions was to expel Satan the Devil and the demons from heaven and restrict their activity to the Earth. (Revelation 12:7-12)

Bible prophecies tell of things to look for like signs, to identify the last days. The Gospel accounts quote Jesus Christ foretelling War, Famine, Great Earthquakes, Disease, Crime, Ruining of the Earth, Deteriorating Attitudes, Breakdown of the Family, Diminished Love of God, Religious Hypocrisy, Increased Understanding of Bible Prophecies, A Global Preaching Work, Widespread Apathy and Ridicule and All Prophecies fulfilled.

Chapter 4 – Revelation

Jesus is Coming and he said to me, "These words are trustworthy and true. And the Lord, the God of the spirits of the prophets, has sent his angle to show his servants what must soon take place." (Revelation 22:6-21) The Bible says that, "Jesus is coming back to reward the inhabitants of the Earth and bring many back to heaven with Him." (Revelation 22:12) Christ will return to Earth at the close of the tribulation. His return from heaven will be personal, visible and glorious, a blessed hope for which we should constantly watch and pray.

Jesus Christ will return. While many claim that we cannot know when He will arrive, the Bible gives us clear signs that will tell us the time is near. We will know that we are approaching that wonderful day when Jesus Christ will return and the seventh trumpet will sound. "Then the seventh angel sounded: And there were loud voices in heaven, saying, "The kingdoms of this world have become the kingdoms of our Lord and of His Christ, and He shall reign forever and ever!"

(Revelation 11:15)

"And there were noises and thundering and lightnings; and there was a great earthquake, such a mighty and great earthquake as had not occurred since men were on the Earth." (Revelation 16:18) "But immediately after the tribulation of these days the sun will be darkened, and the moon will not give its light, and the stars will fall from the sky, and the powers of the heavens will be shaken."

(Revelation 24:29) "And then the sign of the Son of Man will appear in the sky, and then all the tribes of the Earth will mourn, and they will see the Son of Man coming on the clouds of the sky with power and great glory." (Revelation 24:30)

Chapter 5 – Where is Our Hope?

We put our hope in Christ, for there is no other salvation. We put our hope in Christ for the sake of eternity. We put our hope in Christ because we are faithful ambassadors for God. We put our hope in the salvation of Christ alone because there is no other way of salvation. What is our only hope in life and death? That we are not our own but belong to God. Hope is found in the promises God has given us, promises of freedom from sin. We can find so much hope in scripture through the gift of Jesus Christ.

Our hope in God isn't hidden nor outside of our reach. Hoping in God comes with the day by day walking and talking with Him. Hope is restored and renewed. "And hope does not put us to shame, because God's love has been poured into our hearts through the Holy Spirit who has been given to us." (Psalm 33:22) We live now "in hope for eternal life which God, who cannot lie, promised before time began." (Titus 1:2) Since God cannot lie, our hope cannot be in vain. There is only one place that can withstand the weight of our hope, God's Word. God's Word is alive, active and able to transform the hearts of people.

Our hope comes from God. May He fill you with joy and peace because of your trust in Him. May your hope grow stronger by the power of the Holy Spirit. Our hope in God isn't just a wish or a dream, but a sure confidence that what God says will happen. The Bible says that true hope is unseen. And if we can be hopeful for one thing, such as our salvation, which is also unseen, that we can be hopeful for other things too. "For in this hope we were saved. But hope that is seen is no hope at all. Who hopes for what they already have?" (Romans 8:24) "Now faith is confidence in what we hope for and assurance about what we do not see." (Hebrews 11:1) As believers, then we are to live with hope. We are not a people who have hope only in this world; we have hope in the world to come.

Chapter 6 – Future Changes in the World

Our digital world grows; devices will have to expand until your devices can serve you totally. This won't happen overnight. By 2025, Web3 technologies will have revolutionized the world of commerce. By 2030, the world will be more complicated, divided between a broad American sphere of influence in Europe, the Middle East and South Asia, and a Chinese sphere in East Asia and Africa. Today we face many problems, from epidemics to climate change. Grand challenges call for grand ideas, new technology, clever science and smart solutions.

At a social level, we could be heading toward an even greater divide between rich and poor, between the haves and have not's. How predictable are such changes? For example, who could foresee how much mobile technology was to change daily life? Our world is changing fast. Our world was experiencing an extraordinary rate of change before the pandemic and it's only sped up. Artificial intelligence will change the way humans of all ages learn. Big demographic, economic and technological changes are coming. Need for new solutions in a rapidly changing world.

What does the future of globalization look like? New research breaks down changes in the global flows that bind us. Earth will continue to feel ever smaller in 2030; not only are more people able to communicate over the internet. With humanity 90% of the world population will be able to read, 75% will have mobile connectivity, 60% should have broadband access and they will also move to other locations more. Connectivity is not only virtual and digital but also physical. The internet will be in our cars, homes and even on our bodies. By 2030, the number of devices connected to the internet will have reached 125 billion, up from 27 billion in 2017. Humanity is having a devastating impact on the natural world, fuelling dangerous levels of climate change and more turbulent weather.

Chapter 7 – Great Reset

The Great Reset Initiative is an economic recovery plan drawn up by the World Economic Forum in response to the economic and social conditions stemming from the COVID-19 pandemic. The project was launched in June 2020. The world's most influential leaders and thinkers share their ideas for what the future should look like in a post coronavirus world. Now it is up to leaders in the private and public sectors to seize the moment and help create a more equitable and sustainable society. The Great Reset a blueprint of wide-ranging changes meant to lead to a greener and fairer society is gaining momentum. It proposes an ambitious redesign of today's economic system.

The Great Reset concept covers five priorities. First, it envisions a new social contract that fosters social inclusion, decreases the burden passed on to future generations, and reduces inequality within and between countries, defusing social unrest. Second priority is a decarbonization of the economy to fight global warming. Third priority is an intensification of the Fourth Industrial Revolution based on digitalization. Fourth priority is a shift from short-term shareholder capitalism to more equitable and greener longer-term stakeholder capitalism. Fifth priority closer global cooperation, especially on environmental issues, would lead the world out of national isolationism.

The changes we have already seen in response to COVID-19 prove that a reset of our economic and social foundations is possible. It is time to discard approaches to global well being that are broken or ill adapted and to take up dialogue across societies to pursue real progress. History shows that epidemics have been the great resetter of countries economy and social fabric. The pandemic represents a rare but narrow window of opportunity to reflect, reimagine and reset our world. The Great Reset is a commitment to jointly and urgently build the foundations of our economic and social system for a more fair, sustainable and resilient future in response to the COVID-19 pandemic.

Chapter 8 – Acceptance of Jesus Christ

God wants you to have peace and eternal life. What keeps us from the life He planned for us? Our sin separates us from God. Confess your sins and ask God to forgive you. Then ask Jesus to come into your heart and accept Him as your Lord and Savior. Accepting Jesus as your personal Savior means placing your own personal faith and trust in Him. You need to accept Christ as your Lord and Savior in order to restore your relationship with God that has been broken by sin. Jesus, I believe you are the Son of God, that you died on the cross to rescue me from sin and death and to restore me to the Father.

Accepting Jesus into your heart is simply accepting his way of living, loving and leading our lives. For many, it simply means that one must, from the heart, accept Jesus as who the Bible teaches He is, the Son of God and the only Savior. To accept Jesus as your personal Savior is to acknowledge who Jesus is in your own life. It is to believe in Him. "Accepting Jesus Christ as our Savior requires us to believe that salvation is only by Christ alone." (John 14:6) Only Jesus Christ is the one who paid for our sins on the cross.

"Because, if you confess with your mouth that Jesus Christ is Lord and Savior and believe in your heart that God raised Him from the dead, you will be saved."

(Romans 6:23) Welcoming Jesus into your heart is one of the first steps to being a Christian. Accepting Jesus Christ as your Lord and Savior isn't as difficult as you may think. The foundations of salvation; admit that you are a sinner, believe in God and Jesus Christ and confess all of your sins. These foundations can help you grow your faith and invite Jesus Christ into your life. Despite your sinning against Him as much as we do, God loves each one of us so much that he sent His sinless perfect Son, Jesus Christ to die for our sins on the cross. To accept Jesus Christ as your personal Savior is to acknowledge who He is in your own life. It is to believe and trust in Him.

Chapter 9 – Resistance of Jesus Christ

Jesus was never passive and he never used violence. Even before Pilate, he engaged in nonviolent action. The peak of Jesus nonviolent resistance was demonstrated on crucifixion and resurrection in the ultimate example of nonviolent resistance to the empire of violence and death. We do not normally think about Jesus as being resistant to things. He certainly never resisted His heavenly Father nor the Will of God. Jesus provides three examples of nonviolent resistance to evil. Turning the other cheek, giving up one's cloak and walking the second mile.

The Pharisees opposed Jesus because they did not know the direction of the Holy Spirit's work, because they did not know the way of truth spoken. Jesus resisted evil, called the powerful to account and healed the most vulnerable. Jesus did not preach passive acceptance of the oppressive powers. He taught a nonviolent resistance. Jesus often resisted the power structures of his day. Jesus certainly pushed back against evil men especially the religious leaders of the day. He certainly resisted them, at least in terms of confronting them, challenging them, rebuking them and chastising them. He stood his ground against these men, just as he stood strong and resisted the devil during the wilderness temptations.

Jesus Christ response to a violent world as told by Luke. (Luke 6:27-38) The Sermon on the Plain. "But I say to you that listen, Love your enemies, do good to those who hate you, bless those who curse you, pray for those who abuse you. If anyone strikes you on the cheek, offer the other also; and from anyone who takes away your coat do not withhold even your shirt. Give to everyone who begs from you; and if anyone takes away your goods, do not ask for them again. Do to others as you would have them do to you. If you love those who love you, what credit is that to you? For even sinners love those who love them. If you do good to those who do good to you, what credit is that to you? For even sinners do the same. But love your enemies, do good and lend, expecting nothing in return. Your reward will be great, and you will be children of the Most High; for he is kind to the ungrateful and the wicked. Be compassionate, just as your Father is compassionate. Do not judge, and you will not be judged; do not condemn, and you will not be condemned. Forgive, and you will be forgiven."

Chapter 10 - Pathway to Peace

The pathway to peace starts with praise. The pathway to peace also requires prayer. "Do not be anxious about anything, but in every situation, by prayer and petition, with thanksgiving, present your requests to God. And the peace of God, which transcends all understanding, will guard your hearts and your minds in Christ Jesus." (Philippians 4:6-7) Jesus is the only true path to true peace. Run to Jesus, He is your safe harbor in the storm of life. Fear and anxiety happen when we look to the future.

The price of peace is righteousness. Men and nations may loudly proclaim, Peace, peace, but there shall be no peace until individuals nurture in their souls those principles of personal purity, integrity, and character which foster the development of peace. Peace cannot be imposed. It must come from the lives and hearts of men. There is no other way. How have human beings put aside peace? They have rejected Jesus Christ and His message, disregarding the way to reconciliation. Jesus the Prince of Peace was born on Earth to provide for His people a path of peace.

Pathway of peace, living in a growing relationship with Jesus Christ. Why do so many Christians still lack peace? The uncertainties of the world in which we live coupled with the fast pace and stress of daily living leave many people including Christians with anxieties about health, finances, relationships, the future and more. We believe in Jesus and acknowledge He is with us. We know the Bible tells us God has given us His peace and urges us not to worry. Yet many of us still struggle. Is it possible to experience God's peace all the time? A peace born not only from trust in a sovereign God, But also from the assurance that we hope we can hear His voice.

Chapter 11 – Prince of Peace

Jesus Christ is called the Prince of Peace because He is our peace offering. He chose to go to the cross and offer Himself as a sacrifice. Jesus Christ is the only reason we can truly live peacefully with God and He restores every broken relationship. It is a peace that changes us from enemies of God into the children of God. "It pleased the Father by Him to reconcile all things to Himself, by Him, whether things on Earth or things in heaven, having made peace through the blood of His cross. And you, who once were alienated and enemies in your mind by wicked works, yet now He has reconciled." (Colossians 1:19-21) The Prince of Peace has brought to us the opportunity to have peace with God.

The promise for peace found in Isaiah will be brought to fruition through Jesus when he completes His Kingdom. Peace only comes when we are united in Christ. It is the peace of knowing that our future is secured once we accept Jesus as our Savior. That the things of this world are meaningless. Jesus has power over the peace in nature. Jesus being the Prince of Peace means he has control over all types of peace.

The death and resurrection of Jesus was always the plan. God longed to transform our chaotic and hateful world into a world filled with His love. "For to us a child is born, to us a son is given, and the government will be on his shoulders. And he will be called Wonderful Counselor, Mighty God, Everlasting Father and Prince of Peace. Of the greatness of his government and peace there will be no end. He will reign on David's throne and over his kingdom, establishing and upholding it with justice and righteousness from that time on and forever. The zeal of the Lord Almighty will accomplish this." (Isaiah 9:6-7)

Chapter 12 – Good Verse Evil

"Don't let evil conquer you, but conquer evil by doing good." (Romans 12:21) "Keeping a clear conscience, so that those who slander you may be put to shame by your good behavior in Christ." (1 Peter 3:16) Do not let my heart be drawn to what is evil, so that I take part in wicked deeds along with those who are evildoers; do not let me eat their delicacies. In our worldview, there is absolute truth and a clear distinction between good and evil. God's standards don't change, and neither does He.

Jesus gives us the answer in the parable of the good and bad fruits. He tells us to judge a teacher or minister by his or her deeds, not by his or her claims. The true teachings of the Bible will be consistent with the two great themes of the Ten Commandments and the Greatest Commandments of Jesus. Learning the wisdom of the Bible helps us discern good from evil and good teachings from evil teachings. There is no better application for the wisdom of the Bible than to be able to distinguish good from evil, and to practice good in our own lives.

"Do not be overcome by evil, but overcome evil with good." (Romans 12:21) If possible, so far as it depends on you, live peaceably with all. Be loved, never avenge yourselves, but leave it to the wrath of God. "But the Lord is faithful, and He will strengthen you and protect you from the evil one." (2 Thessalonians 3:3) The Bible assures believers that God's promise of the ultimate triumph of good over evil will be fulfilled. Jesus Christ, the Son of God, is sovereign even over demons. The Lord Jesus Christ is sovereign even over the forces of evil.

Chapter 13 – Jesus has Overcome the World

"I have told you these things, so that in me you may have peace. In this world you will have trouble. But take Heart! I have overcome the world." (John 16:33) I have told you all this so that you may have peace in me. Here on Earth you will have many trials and sorrows. Remember Jesus promise to our troubled hearts in this world. When Jesus walked the Earth he was a man of sorrows.

"For whatever is born of God overcomes the world; and this is the victory that has overcome the world – our faith." (1 John 5:4) Who is it that overcomes the world? Only he who believes that Jesus is the Son of God. Speaking to the Apostles in His final moments before Gethsemane, Jesus said, "In the world ye shall have tribulation, but be of good cheer; I have overcome the world."

(John 16:33) For everyone born of God is victorious and overcomes the world; and this is the victory that has conquered and overcome the world our faith.

Jesus Christ who has already defeated death. Jesus knew exactly what was coming. He had tried to warn his disciples ahead of time that he would be arrested, tried, falsely accused and crucified. And he also explained he would return after these ordeals. But they just couldn't understand. The born-again believers are not of the world; however, they live in the world that is hostile to the cause of Jesus Christ and His followers. Anyone who puts his faith in the person of Jesus Christ and His finished redemptive work becomes a partaker in Christ's victory over the world and its lusts. Through death, Jesus conquered the world, and because of this, we can have hope.

Chapter 14 – God's Law

The law of God is first understood in terms of who God is as the Creator and Lord. Then in its covenantal context of instruction for God's people. God's law gives direction, wisdom and joy to our lives. Yet we know that a person is not justified by works of the law but through faith in Jesus Christ. The law reflects the character of God. It reveals His holiness, righteousness and love. Through the law, we gain insight in to God's nature.

The law is God's perfect standard of obedience and holiness as described in the commands, statutes and ordinances given to those who would worship and serve Him. "The very first law was given in the Garden of Eden when God told Adam not to eat of the tree of the knowledge of good and evil." (Genesis 2:16-17) God's commands are His laws. "While the Law generally refers to the Ten Commandments and the sacrificial laws given to Moses on Mount Sinai."

(Exodus 20) God gave instructions to men long before the children of Israel left Egypt as a nation.

God's law is the spiritual law that we have in the New Testament and it is the covenant between God and Israel. The law is not a burden to the Christian because Jesus fulfilled the law on our behalf. His obedience has replaced our disobedience. We have the freedom to choose to obey the laws upon which blessings are predicated, and enjoy those blessings or we can choose to ignore the laws and face the consequences.

Chapter 15 – Jesus the Redeemer

Let not your heart be troubled; you believe in God, believe also in me. Jesus who gave himself for us to redeem us from all wickedness. Thus says the Lord, your Redeemer, the Holy One of Israel: "I am the Lord your God, who teaches you to profit, who leads you in the way you should go." (Isaiah 48:17) Throughout the Bible, God's work of redemption points to Jesus as the supreme Redeemer of humanity. Why should you ever want to doubt your salvation yet again?

As for me, I know that my redeemer lives, and at the last He will take His stand on the Earth. "So they will fear the name of the LORD from the west And His glory from the rising of the sun, For He will come like a rushing stream which the wind of the LORD drives. A Redeemer will come to Zion, And to those who turn from transgression in Jacob." declares the LORD. (Isaiah 59:19-20) Jesus died for our sins; He redeemed us from the curse of sin; He forgives our sins; He gives us gifts; and He leads us to glory.

Jesus Christ gave himself for us, that he might redeem us from all iniquity. Jesus Christ washed us from our sins in his own blood.

I have blotted out your transgressions like a cloud and your sins like mist. Jesus Christ redeems believers from all forms of sinful bondage and oppression through his death and resurrection. The only Redeemer is the Lord Jesus Christ, the eternal Son of God, in whom God became man and bore the penalty for sin himself.

Chapter 16 – Light of the World

"I am the Light of the world." (John 8:12) This is the second of seven "I am" declarations of Jesus, recorded only in John's gospel, that point to His unique divine identity and purpose. In declaring Himself to be the Light of the world, Jesus was claiming that He is the exclusive source of spiritual light. No other source of spiritual truth is available to mankind. Jesus casts out darkness and calls us to do the same through faith and obedience.

God is the light that shines within and through His church as the light of the world. Jesus Christ has many names and titles. One of them is "Light of the World." He taught, "I am the light of the world: he that followeth me shall not walk in darkness, but shall have the light of life." (John 8:12) Jesus gives us the truth about God and about life, our origin and our destiny. Jesus being "the light of the world" means the world has no other light than Him.

Jesus Christ is also the light of the world because his power persuades us to do good and his unity and union with the father. Jesus Christ was born to be a light to the world. Jesus tells us that He has come into this world as a light and those that believe in

Him have been brought out of the darkness. Jesus came into this world to be the Light of the world, and to point the world towards God. Jesus Christ is called Immanuel which means God with us.

Chapter 17 – Unseen Eternity

"So we fix our eyes not on what is seen, but on what is unseen, for what is seen is temporary, but what is unseen is eternal." (2 Corinthians 4:18) The invisible God is eternal, outside of time. Whatever exists with Him in the spiritual world will never end. "Our light and momentary troubles are achieving for us an eternal glory that far outweighs them all." (2 Corinthians 4:17) "So we do not, lose heart. Though our outer self is wasting away, our inner self is being renewed day by day." (2 Corinthians 4:16)

The Bible tells us that the future extends beyond Earth. When we die and leave this Earth, we will spend eternity in Heaven. "The son is the image of the invisible God, the first born over all creation." (Colossians 1:15) Being a Christian is about coming to Jesus Christ for eternal life. Living for eternity in our minds will change the focus of our life, from the world to eternity in Heaven. Jesus Christ as Lord, and ourselves as your servants for Jesus sake.

There will come a day when we will realize that the stressful, worried hours we spent on the temporary Earth were a waste of time. Eternal kingdom that awaits all who follow Christ. This is the essence of faith. What are these unseen things? They are the resources of the grace of God. We need to ask God to open our eyes to what is at stake, to the unseen world and the reality of Heaven, our eternal destination. Look confidently at unseen, eternal things. The invisible is eternal, inward and an unseen treasure. You have the most powerful message in the world. Discover your purpose, live with an eternal perspective.

Chapter 18 – Anti-Christ Rises

In Christian religion, the Antichrist refers to people prophesied by the Bible to oppose Jesus Christ and substitute themselves in Christ's place before the Second Coming. The term Antichrist is found four times in the New Testament in the Book of John. The meaning of Antichrist is one who denies or opposes Christ, a great antagonist expected to fill the world with wickedness. The Antichrist will forge a one-world government through promises of peace. But when Jesus returns, he will expose the Antichrist as an impostor, defeat him in the battle of Armageddon, and reign with the Christian martyrs for a thousand years on Earth.

The Antichrist is a tempter who works by signs and wonders and seeks divine honors. In the End Times, a man will come who will be the devil in the flesh. The Bible calls him the Beast, the son of perdition, the man of lawlessness and the Antichrist. The Apostle John wrote of his vision, "I saw a beast rising up out of the sea." (Revelation 13:1b) The sea stands for the nations of the world. The Beast will come suddenly in a time when nations are in turmoil. "Now the beast which I saw was like a leopard, his feet were like the feet of a bear, and his mouth like the mouth of a lion." (Revelation 13:2a) The lion, bear and leopard represent world empires. The lion represents Babylon, the bear represents Medo-Persia, and the leopard represents Greece and Alexander the Great's rapid world conquest. "I saw a beast rising up out of the sea, having seven heads and ten horns, and on his horns ten crowns, and on his heads a blasphemous name." (Revelation 13:1b)

Apostle Paul uses his word to inform us that a day is coming when the Antichrist who has been concealed and hidden from public view will suddenly appear. The Antichrist is satanically inspired and sets himself up as God. At some point in the future the Antichrist is going to step onto the platform of the world stage through the sea of politics and take the leading role for a short time in the affairs of mankind. The real Antichrist is still yet to be revealed in the last days. "Let no man deceive you by any means: for that day shall not come, except there come a falling away first, and that man of sin be revealed, the son of perdition; who opposeth and exalteth himself above all that is called God, or that is worshipped; so that he as God sitteth in the temple of God, showing himself that he is God."

(2 Thessalonians 2:3-4)

Chapter 19 – False Prophets

In the Sermon on the Mount, Jesus warns his followers of false prophets. "Beware of false prophets, who come to you in sheep's clothing but inwardly are ravenous wolves. You will know them by their fruits. Are grapes gathered from thorns, or figs from thistles?" (Matthew 7:15-20) A false prophet is a person who falsely claims the gift of prophecy or divine inspiration, or to speak for God, or who makes such claims for evil ends. False prophets and false teachers are those who arrogantly attempt to fashion new interpretations of the scriptures to demonstrate that these sacred texts should not be read as God's words to His children but merely as the utterances of uninspired men, limited by their own prejudices and cultural biases.

Scripture says to "test the spirits to see whether they are from God, for many false prophets have gone out into the world." (1 John 4:1) "Therefore this is what the Sovereign Lord says: Because of your false words and lying visions, I am against you, declares the Sovereign Lord." (Ezekiel 13:8) Warnings against false prophets: then the word of the Lord came to me. He said, "Son of man, you must speak to the prophets of Israel for me. They are only saying what they want to say. You must speak to them. Tell them this: 'Listen to this message from the Lord!' This is what the Lord God says. "Bad things will happen to you foolish prophets. You are following your own spirits. You are not telling people what you really see in visions." (Ezekiel 13:2-3)

"Thus says the Lord God, Woe to the foolish prophets who follow their own spirit, and have seen nothing! Your prophets have been like jackals among ruins, O Israel." (Ezekiel 13:3-4) God offers instruction on how His people can determine true from false prophets. God explains, "If what a prophet proclaims in the name of the Lord does not take place or come true, that is a message the Lord has not spoken. That prophet has spoken presumptuously, so do not be alarmed."

(Deuteronomy 18:22) The bottom line is that false prophets bring a message that is not from God. Their message contradicts what God instructs, often appealing to our Earthly cravings or passions. Ultimately they produce bad fruit.

Chapter 20 – Mark of the Beast

"And I stood upon the sand of the sea, and saw a beast rise up out of the sea, having seven heads and ten horns and upon his horns ten crowns, and upon his heads the name of blasphemy." (Revelation 3:1) The mark of the beast refers to the name or number of the first beast. That number is 666, according to Revelation 13:18. This beast is usually identified as the Antichrist. This mark is first mentioned in (Revelation 13:16-17) where it is imposed on humanity by the beast out of the Earth.

The human leader of this revived empire is also referred to as the beast. The mark of the beast is the mark or identifying sign of this empire. The Book of Revelation explains that the dragon gives the beast its power and authority. This dragon is Satan the devil. Satan uses the beast to rule and deceive the world. The mark of the beast thus represents disobedience to God's commandments and rejection of the faith of Jesus. The Book of Revelation says that, "Those who receive the mark will be subject to the seven last plagues, while the obedient saints are described as having attained victory over the beast." (Revelation 15:2) "These faithful people will be given eternal life and reign with Christ at His second coming." (Revelation 20:4)

The four beasts of the Book of Daniel 7 are depicted as part of the Antichrist or the beast, because the papacy incorporated pagan beliefs and practices from all four empires. "And that no one may buy or sell except one who has the mark or the name of the beast, or the number of his name." (Revelation 13:17) The receiving of the mark of the beast commands the wrath and indignation of God; and the consequences are severe.

Chapter 21 – Hidden Battle

The hidden battle of the Christian and Christians are engaged in a hidden battle for our very souls. God will go before you to fight your battles. Sometimes God will simply run a protective shield around you where nothing will be able to get through to attack you. That God will fight our battles means we do not have to anguish, be anxious or be discouraged when bad things happen in our lives.

Therefore, let us maintain a strong relationship with Jesus Christ and allow Him to continue to fight our spiritual and emotional battles. We don't have to strive to get victory; we already have it in Jesus Christ. In the scriptures, Armageddon is used symbolically to depict the destruction which God will execute on the spiritual and physical realms of Satan's empire. Therefore, prepare your minds for action, keep sober in spirit, fix your hope completely on the grace to be brought to you at the revelation of Jesus Christ.

Christ fought for us on the cross. This leads us to praise God. God, we praise you for fighting for us. Jesus, we praise you for dying on the cross for us. The Word of God is not to be hidden, but rather used to fight sin and point people to Jesus. Finally God our Father and Jesus Christ our Lord and Savior and the Holy Spirit are to be honored and thanked above all and in all.

Chapter 22 – End of the Age

The phrase "the end of the age" recurs in Matthew 13:39 and 24:3, which describes Jesus teachings about the end of times. This phrase refers to the end of this present era. "Teaching them to observe all that I commanded you; and lo, I am with you always, even to the end of the age." (Matthew 28:20) The end of the age, the end of the world, and the return of Jesus. All these things have taken up residence in believers minds.

End of the age refers to the time of Jesus Christ's second coming and the resurrection of the dead when God will reap the first fruits of His harvest. "As he sat on the Mount of Olives, the disciples came to him privately, saying, "Tell us, when will these things be, and what will be the sign of your coming and of the end of the age?" (Matthew 24:3) Jesus Christ will restore his faithful people to life, purge his enemies from his world, and establish the new heavens and the new Earth as his permanent Kingdom.

"Every eye will see Him." (Revelation 1:7) It will be a universal revelation. While there will be clouds and the sun and the moon may be blotted out temporarily, the heavens will become alive with the brilliant glory, brighter than the light of day when Jesus Christ comes back in power and great glory. If you have eyes to see, you can recognize that our world is approaching a major turning point in the history of human civilization. Jesus Christ knew the ultimate result of the terrible state of affairs men would bring on themselves in this end of the age. It is called the age of chaos for obvious reasons.

Chapter 23 – Nation Against Nation

"And you will hear of wars and rumors of wars. See that you are not alarmed, for this must take place, but the end is not yet." (Revelation 16:6) "For nation shall rise against nation, and kingdom against kingdom: and there shall be famines, and pestilences, and earthquakes in various places." (Matthew 24:7) When nation will rise against nation, and kingdom against kingdom, this meant that the end of the age had begun. Jerusalem is definitely at the center of geopolitics and stands alone against many enemies.

"For I will gather all nations against Jerusalem to battle; and the city shall be taken, and the houses rifled, and the women ravished; and half of the city shall go forth into captivity, and the residue of the people shall not be cut off from the city. Then shall the Lord go forth, and fight against those nations, as when he fought in the day of battle." (Zechariah 14:2-3) At the very moment of the second coming of our Lord all nations shall be gathered against Jerusalem to battle.

The Lord has said, "Every Kingdom divided against itself is brought to desolation; and every city or house divided against itself shall not stand." (Matthew 12:25) The Bible teaches us that there are two unseen kingdoms; the kingdom of light, ruled by God and the kingdom of darkness, ruled by Satan. Nation rising against nation and kingdom against kingdom is a very real conflict and differentiates from the ordinary wars and rumors of wars that are the normalcy of history.

Chapter 24 – Shofar from Heaven

Indeed, Jesus Himself will blow a shofar on the day of rapture. For the Lord himself will descend from heaven with a rousing cry of command. The call of the shofar as a summons to the heavenly court on the Day of Judgment. As a call to the Jewish remnant to come home. As a reminder of the resurrection of Jesus Christ. When Christians blow the shofar, it is a wake-up call for the Jewish and it brings heaven down to Earth.

"For the Lord, Himself will descend from heaven with a shout, with the voice of an archangel, and with the trumpet of God. And the dead in Christ will rise first. Then we who are alive and remain shall be caught up together with them in the clouds to meet the Lord in the air. And thus we shall always be with the Lord. Therefore comfort one another with these words." (1 Thessalonians 4:16-18)

For the Lord himself will descend from heaven with a cry of command, with the voice of an archangel and with the sound of the trumpet of God. The sound of the shofar, a ram's horn, is the bridge between heaven and Earth. For the believer in Jesus, the blast of the shofar represents the shout of God's victory over the power of sin and death. The sound of the shofar was used to warn the people to repent and turn to God to stop judgment from coming on the people because of their iniquity.

Chapter 25 – Breaking of the Seven Seals

The seven seals represent events to take place on this Earth during each seal's specific time period beginning at the time of Christ and continuing until Christ's second coming. The seven seals list are White horse, Red horse, Black horse, Pale horse, Souls crying out from under the altar, Earthquake, sun and moon, stars fall, and Silence in heaven. Seal judgments two through four represent the disintegration of both human civilization and creation resulting from their rejection of the Lamb of God.

In John's vision, the seven seals hold a closed scroll in heaven, and as each seal is broken, a new judgment is unleashed on the Earth. The first four seals unleash the four horsemen of the apocalypse. The second seal releases a rider atop a red horse and wielding a sword. The seven trumpets of the seventh seal show the timeline of Jerusalem. The seven trumpets reveal seven major events in the history of Jerusalem. During the end times, seven year tribulation, God will pour out His wrath as judgment for the world's sin and as a final call for humanity to repent and worship Him.

The seven seals and seven trumpets are a series of catastrophic events that will take place during the End Days to enact the judgment of God upon the Earth. "The seventh seal represents silence. When He opened the seventh seal, there was silence in heaven for about half an hour." (Revelation 8:1) The breaking of the seventh seal occurs in Revelation 8 and marks the second wave of judgments. When the last seal is broken it will be clear what side God takes in all the affairs of Earth. God will judge according to the holiness of His character.

Chapter 26 – Rapture

The word rapture appears nowhere in the New Testament. In his first letter to the Thessalonians, the Apostle Paul wrote that, "The Lord will come down from heaven and that a trumpet call will precede the rise of "the dead in Christ." (1Thessalonians 4:16) "Since you have kept my command to endure patiently, I will also keep you from the hour of trial that is going to come on the whole world to test the inhabitants of the Earth." (Revelation 3:10)

"At that time Michael, the great prince who protect your people, will arise. There will be a time of distress such as has not happened from the beginning of nations until then. But at that time your people – everyone whose name is found written in the book – will be delivered." (Daniel 12:1) "Multitudes who sleep in the dust of the Earth will awake: some to everlasting life, others to shame and everlasting contempt." (Daniel 12:2) "In a flash, in the twinkling of an eye, at the last trumpet. For the trumpet will sound, the dead will be raised imperishable, and we will be changed." (1 Corinthians 15:52)

If a believer is alive at the time of the rapture, they will be taken up with Christ, and their body will be transformed into their glorified bodies. The Rapture is the Biblical prophetic event where all who have put their trust in Christ, living and deceased, will suddenly be caught up from Earth, be joined with Christ in the air, and taken to heaven. Paul describes the Rapture in (1 Thessalonians 4:13-18). Before Jesus Christ establishes His Kingdom on Earth, Jesus will come for His Church, an event commonly referred to as the Rapture.

Chapter 27 – Tribulation

The tribulation is a future seven year period when God will finish His discipline of Israel and finalize His judgment of the unbelieving. "For then there will be great tribulation, such as has not been since the beginning of the world until this time, no, nor ever shall be. And unless those days were shortened, no flesh would be saved; but for the elect's sake those days will be shortened." (Matthew 24:21-22) In his vision, the Apostle John declared, "The great day of His wrath has come, and who is able to stand?" (Revelation 6:17)

Scripture explains that God has great long-suffering with humanity before His anger reaches such a critical point. The tribulation will reveal the depravity of humanity and the justness of God's wrath on the sinful human race. Life in this broken and fallen world can slam each of us to the ground. Before life comes apart totally, let us learn to cling to our only sure foundation with God. The Bible tells over and over again of dark days to come, days of the wrath of God, when Satan will rule on Earth.

"For verily, when we were with you, we told you before that we should suffer tribulation; even as it came to pass, and ye know." (1 Thessalonians 3:4) "These things I have spoken unto you, that in me ye might have peace. In the world ye shall have tribulation: but be of good cheer; I have overcome the world."

(John 16:33) "Because thou hast kept the word of my patience, I also will keep thee from the hour of temptation, which shall come upon all the world, to try them that dwell upon the earth." (Revelation 3:10) "Who shall separate us from the love of Christ? Shall tribulation, or distress, or persecution, or famine, or nakedness, or peril, or sword?" (Romans 8:35)

Chapter 28 – Holy One Verse Satan

Satan enjoys perverting the Bible doctrine and using it to drive a wedge between believers and their Lord. God's Word describes to us in detail who Satan is, his nature, his acts, and his future. The only way to resist the devil is by submitting and drawing near to God. The devil said, "If you will bow down and worship me, I will give you all these things." Jesus said to him, "Get away from me, Satan! The Scriptures say, 'You must worship the Lord your God. Serve only Him!" (Matthew 4:9-10)

"Then Jesus was led up by the spirit into the wilderness to be tempted by the devil. And when He has fasted forty days and forty nights, afterward He was hungry. Now when the tempter came to Him, he said, "If you are the Son of God, command that these stones become bread." But He answered and said, "It is written, 'Man shall not live by bread alone, but by every word that proceeds from the mouth of God." (Matthew 4:1-4)

Believers can still overcome even Satan's limited power, for James 4:7 commands us, "Resist the devil, and he will flee from you." (Revelation 12:11) Revelation 20 is the only place in the Bible that speaks of "the millennium" the thousand-year reign of the triumphant Christ on Earth. Father, I rejoice that because I am in Christ, I am the blessed of the Lord and protected by the blood of Jesus Christ.

Chapter 29 – Fall of the Beast

The beast cannot touch God in Heaven, nor the Saints who have already gone to Heaven, so he is reduced to name calling. In Revelation 13 John sees a nightmare vision of a dragon and two beasts. The first beast comes out of the sea and receives power from the dragon or Satan. The second beast comes from the land which is a false prophet. The second beast's role is to bring people to worship the first beast and promote his aims, who is a proxy of the devil.

"The beast that thou sawest was, and is not; and shall ascend out of the bottomless pit, and go into perdition: and they that dwell on the earth shall wonder, whose names were not written in the book of life from the foundation of the world, when they behold the beast that was, and is not, and yet is."

(Revelation 17:8) "These have one mind, and shall give their power and strength unto the beast. These shall make war with the Lamb, and the Lamb shall overcome them: for he is Lord of lords, and King of kings: and they that are with him are called, and chosen, and faithful." (Revelation 17:13-14)

"And the beast was captured, and with it the false prophet who in its presence had done the signs by which he deceived those who had received the mark of the beast and those who worshiped its image. These two were thrown alive into the lake of fire that burns with sulfur." (Revelation 19:20) "He seized the dragon, that ancient serpent, who is the devil, or Satan, and bound him for a thousand years. He threw him into the Abyss, and locked and sealed it over him, to keep him from deceiving the nations anymore until the thousand years were ended. After that, he must be set free for a short time." (Revelation 20:2-3)

Chapter 30 – New Jerusalem

"New Jerusalem is fully illuminated by the glory of God and the light of the Lamb brightens the city." (Revelation 2:23) There is no need for the Sun or Mon. "Then I saw a new heaven and a new earth, for the first heaven and the first earth had passed away and there was no longer any sea. I saw the Holy City, the new Jerusalem, coming down out of heaven from God, prepared as a bride beautifully dressed for her husband." (Revelation 21:1-2)

"He will wipe away every tear from their eyes, and death shall be no more, neither shall there be mourning, nor crying, nor pain anymore, for the former things have passed away." (Revelation 21:4) "And I heard a loud voice from the throne saying, "Behold, the dwelling place of God is with man. He will dwell with them, and they will be his people, and God himself will be with them as their God." (Revelation 21:3) "In my Father's house are many rooms. If it were not so, would I have told you that I go to prepare a place for you? And if I go and prepare a place for you, I will come again and will take you to myself, that where I am you may be also." (John 14:2-3)

"The one who conquers, I will make him a pillar in the temple of my God. Never shall he go out of it, and I will write on him the name of my God, and name of the city of my God, the new Jerusalem, which comes down from my God out of heaven, and my own new name." (Revelation 3:12) "But be glad and rejoice forever in that which I create; for behold, I create Jerusalem to be a joy, and her people to be a gladness. I will rejoice in Jerusalem and be glad in my people; no more shall be heard in it the sound of weeping and the cry of distress."

(Isaiah 65:18-19)

"By its light will the nations walk, and the kings of the earth will bring their glory into it, and its gates will never be shut by day – and there will be no night there. They will bring into it the glory and the honor of the nations."

(Revelation 21:24-26) "And he carried me away in the Spirit to a great, high mountain, and showed me the holy city Jerusalem coming down out of heaven from God, having the glory of God, its radiance like a most rare jewel, like a jasper, clear as crystal. It had a great, high wall, with twelve gates, and at the gates twelve gates, and on the gates the names of the twelve tribes of the sons of Israel were inscribed. (Revelation 21:10-12)

"And I saw the holy city, New Jerusalem, coming down out of heaven from God, prepared as a bride adorned for her husband." (Revelation 21:2) "And the wall of the city had twelve foundations, and on them were the twelve names of the twelve apostles of the Lamb." (Revelation 21:14) "But you have come to Mount Zion and to the city of the living God, the heavenly Jerusalem, and to innumerable angels in festal gathering." (Hebrews 12:22) "No longer will there be anything accursed, but the throne of God and of the Lamb will be in it, and his servants will worship him. They will see his face, and his name will be on their foreheads."

(Revelation 22:3-4)

I leave you with these scriptures. "I am with you always, even unto the end of the world." (Matthew 28:20) "The LORD appeared to me (Israel) from ages past, saying, "I have loved you with an everlasting love, Therefore with lovingkindness I have drawn you and continued My faithfulness to you." (Jeremiah 31:3)

Chapter 31 – Author Living Testimony

How God Changed My Life

My living testimony with how God changed my life. My new life began when I was baptized a second time with my wife at Calvary Christian Church in Virginia. Mega and I were baptized together and then decided to become self-supporting missionaries in Indonesia in the year 2008. We arrived in the country and then began ministering at a local church and my wife is an evangelist. Within a year we started American English for Life – English Language Center Education Ministry which is also a group on Facebook.

During the sixteen years that we have been in Indonesia, we have taught English to more than 2,500 students and we are teaching English to this day. My wife and I teach all grade levels all the way up to doctors. We have taught sixty seminary students for two months for free and many other students at large discounted fees. This is our way of giving back for God's grace in our lives. Today we only teach English by receiving love gifts. We are now preparing to start a house of prayer combined with our English Education Ministry.

We have lived in Indonesia at twelve different locations all over the country. Being there are 17,508 islands in Indonesia the largest archipelago in the world with many more locations that we can teach at to help people to learn English. My wife and I want to teach English to as many students as we can in different areas of the country.

Our feelings about missionary responsibilities are very important to us in our lives. God gives every one of us a unique mission and he gives us a choice as to whether or not we fulfill that mission. We were made for a mission, and that mission gives our life meaning. The Bible says, "God has made us what we are. I Christ Jesus, God made us to do good works, which God planned in advance for us to live our lives doing." (Ephesians 2:10)

In other words, we are unique. No one else in the whole world – past, present, or future – is like us. God has made us so unique that there are certain things only we can contribute to the world. Those things make up our life mission. Until we knew our life mission, we were just existing. To experience the fulfillment in our lives we are living out God's intentions for us. Jesus says in (Mark 8:35), "If you insist on saving your life, you will lose it. Only those who throw away their lives for my sake and for the sake of the Good News will ever know what it means to really live."

God is giving us the opportunity to build our lives around His mission for us. The only way to do that is by starting with a firm foundation with Jesus Christ. "And no one can ever lay any other real foundation than that one we already have – Jesus Christ." (1 Corinthians 3:11) We can choose to build our lives on Jesus, the only foundation that will last. Or we can choose to spend our lives chasing things that ultimately will fail us.

What is certain is that one day we will stand before God and He will ask us: "Did you fulfill the mission that I gave you on this Earth?" On that day, it will be clear whether we spent our lives fulfilling God's mission for us or we chose to chase lesser things. A step of faith for our God given mission will test our faith. It may challenge our comfort zones. It may challenge our prejudices. But we can't accomplish God's mission for our lives without faith. "Without faith it is impossible to please God, because anyone who comes to him must believe that he exists and that he rewards those who earnestly seek him." (Hebrews 11:6)

God will be with us every step along our mission, guiding and providing for us. Jesus promised this when he gave the Great Commission. "Therefore go and make disciples of all nations, baptizing them in the name of the Father and of the Son and of the Holy Spirit, and teaching them to obey everything I have commanded you. And surely I am with you always, to the very end of the age."

(Matthew 28:19-20)